# *Christmas*

## PAPER CRAFTING

### Holiday Cards, Gift Tags, AND More!

**DESIGN ORIGINALS**
an Imprint of Fox Chapel Publishing
www.d-originals.com

# Welcome

## to a wealth of Christmas papercrafting!

This book provides you with ready-made papercrafting materials that will add a burst of holiday spirit to your home, your gifts, and your mood. However, the extra-special thing about the crafting elements in this book is that although they're beautiful as standalone pieces, they also offer a ton of flexibility to add your own personal, inspired touches! You can use your own words, embellish with other crafting materials, and combine cards with scrapbook paper designs to create beautiful pieces. Pick the color schemes you like and the sentiments that speak to you, and let the creativity flow!

# Project Ideas

# Crafting Materials

# CRAFTED CARDS

Craft a heartfelt card for any recipient by pulling your favorite art cards from this book and adding all kinds of fun embellishments. Layer with scrapbook papers, add gemstones and glitter, use 3-dimensional glue dots to add some height to your card... the possibilities are endless when sending a positive Christmas message to everyone you know!

The art cards and accompanying scrapbook paper cards in this book come in a variety of sizes and backings. You can cut the border off of the smaller art cards and mount the art on top of a scrapbook paper card so that it creates a new border; you can paste a scrapbook paper card to the back of an art card back to back and write your own sentiment on the colored side; or you can simply embellish an existing art card and give it to a friend. Experiment with different combinations!

Don't forget to check out the **colorable cards** on pages 55–60 as well as the ready-to-roll **foldable cards** on pages 49–54!

*The large envelope on page 79 is a standard size and should be happily accepted and mailed at your local post office.*

# CRAFTED ENVELOPES

The envelope is a very important facet of card giving, so why settle for plain, uninspired envelopes when you could have completely personalized, prettily patterned homes for your cards to travel in? Before you start, remove the envelope templates on pages 77–80. Laminate the templates or paste them to thick poster board to ensure your templates live a long, healthy life of envelope shaping.

## How to Assemble an Envelope

*1.* Trace your master envelope template onto your favorite piece of double-sided scrapbook paper (see pages 77–80). Cut out the newly traced template and set your master template aside.

*2.* Referring to the dashed lines on your master template, create the shape of the envelope by first folding the two side flaps in toward the center, then folding in the bottom flap. Double check the way you're folding so your favorite scrapbook pattern is on the outside of the envelope and the accent color is on the inside.

*3.* Tape the bottom three folded flaps of the envelope together, leaving the top flap free to open and close. If you plan to hand deliver your envelope to its recipient, feel free to only tape on the inside, where the tape will be hidden. If you want to mail your crafted envelope, add extra tape on the outside seams of the flaps to ensure that the envelope doesn't come open in transit.

*4.* Insert your completed card, add your destination to the front in some fancy script, stick on a stamp, and off it goes!

# CRAFTED GIFT TAGS

Like envelopes, gift tags are essential to gift giving. How else are we supposed to identify which perfectly wrapped parcel goes to which perfectly picked friend? In this book you will find 16 gift tags (see pages 69–72) ready to be cut out, crafted up, and sent packing.

Just like the cards, these gift tags are lovely enough to stand alone but can become mini masterpieces with just a few added elements. The same ribbons, gemstones, and layered effects you can use to make cards can be used for the tags to create the most magnificent gift set.

Don't be afraid to embellish! Add hand lettering and bling, or even tie a cute charm to a gift tag.

Jessica

MERRY MISTLETOE
SCENTED CANDLE

>> I ♡ this part!

baby
its
COLD
outside

Merry Christmas

# CRAFTED BOOKMARKS

What could be cozier during the holiday season than curling up with a good book by a crackling fire? Ensure you never lose your place by keeping a holly jolly bookmark between the pages of your book. Add a personal touch to your bookmarks by including notes on the back of them, and then, perhaps, by making your own tassels!

ALL is CALM
ALL IS
Bright

## How to Make a Mini Tassel

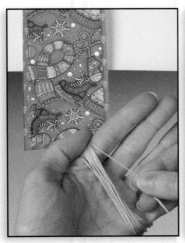

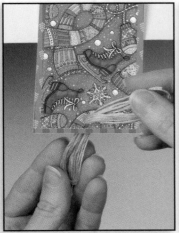

*1.* Punch a hole in the bookmark. Wrap your chosen yarn/twine/embroidery floss evenly and snugly around the width of your palm.

*2.* Slide the wrapped bundle off of your palm, keeping it flat and intact. Thread the bundle through the hole, then fold it to bring the two halves together.

*3.* Tie a piece of yarn tightly around the entire bundle, right at the edge of the bookmark. You can wrap the piece of yarn around the bundle multiple times before tying it.

*4.* Cut the top of all the loops to create the fringe. Fluff the fringe and trim it as desired, being sure to also trim the piece of yarn used to tie the bundle.

Merry Christmas to all and to all a good night!
—'Twas the Night Before Christmas

Here we come a-caroling!

All the world is happy when Santa Claus comes.
—Maud Lindsay

Every time a bell rings, an angel gets his wings.
—It's a Wonderful Life

# CRAFTED MINI CARDS

In this book you will find a collection of mini cards that have been beautifully illustrated with holiday imagery and inspiring sentiments. Laminate them for your wallet as a reminder of what the Christmas season is all about or to share with a friend, or perhaps make some DIY fridge magnets with them! You never know when you might need to share a little Yuletide joy, and these mini cards are a perfect reminder that it's the season of warmth, love, and family. If you don't have a laminator, use clear packing tape to laminate your mini cards right at home with little to no fuss.

At Christmas, all roads lead home.
—Marjorie Holmes

## How to Make a Fridge Magnet

*1.* Collect your materials. You will need your favorite mini cards from this book, a few sheets of mat board, glue, adhesive magnets (dots or strips), a container of Mod Podge Dimensional Magic Glaze or similar product, and a container of regular Mod Podge decoupage medium (matte or glossy) or similar product.

*2.* Cut the mat board to the size you want your magnet. Cut out and glue a piece of scrapbook paper to the mat board, ensuring that all of the corners are completely adhered. Glue a mini card on top of the scrapbook paper.

*3.* Use the decoupage medium to cover the entire face of the magnet, starting with the outside perimeter and filling in.* Use the glaze to accent select areas of the mini card. Use a straight pin or safety pin to pop any bubbles that may form in the glaze. (Putting glaze all over the entire magnet may cause it to warp.)

*4.* After the glaze has dried completely, attach your magnets to the reverse side. Voilà: you are on your way to transforming your fridge into a winter wonderland!

*\*Sealing your entire magnet with decoupage medium is a good idea because it helps protect your magnet from fridge spills and makes it more durable for repeatedly taking it off the fridge to pin new things.*

# CRAFTED FRAMEABLES

A popular, classic, and effortless way to fill your home with the Christmas spirit is with framed art. Placing a beautifully colored picture or inspiring holiday quote in an eye-catching frame will always be a genuine way to spread cheer, whether it's for your home or a gift for a loved one. Take it one step further by jazzing up your frame with embellishments like stickers, ribbons, or hand lettering.

# Ready, Set, Craft!

On the following pages you'll find everything you need to make gorgeous crafts—perforated, colored, and all ready for you! Just go for it and don't stress about whether you're doing it "right." Pour your soul into your work, and the result will be beautiful! Enjoy!

_____
_____
_____
_____
_____
_____
_____
_____

*Christmas waves a magic wand over this
world, and behold, everything is softer
and more beautiful.*

—Norman Vincent Peale

_____
_____
_____
_____
_____

*Christmas waves a magic wand over this
world, and behold, everything is softer
and more beautiful.*

—Norman Vincent Peale

_____
_____
_____
_____
_____
_____
_____
_____

*Each sight, each sound of Christmas*
*And fragrances sublime*
*Make hearts and faces happy*
*This glorious Christmastime.*

*—Carice William*

_____
_____
_____
_____
_____

*Each sight, each sound of Christmas*
*And fragrances sublime*
*Make hearts and faces happy*
*This glorious Christmastime.*

*—Carice William*

_____
_____
_____
_____
_____
_____
_____

*It's the most wonderful time of the year*
*There'll be much mistletoeing*
*And hearts will be glowing*
*When loved ones are near*
*It's the most wonderful time of the year*

*—Edward Pola and George Wyle,*
*"It's the Most Wonderful Time of the Year"*

_____
_____
_____
_____
_____

*It's the most wonderful time of the year*
*There'll be much mistletoeing*
*And hearts will be glowing*
*When loved ones are near*
*It's the most wonderful time of the year*

*—Edward Pola and George Wyle,*
*"It's the Most Wonderful Time of the Year"*

_____
_____
_____
_____
_____
_____
_____
_____

*Oh the weather outside is frightful, but the fire is so delightful, and since we've no place to go, let it snow! Let it snow! Let it snow!*

—*"Let It Snow"*

_____
_____
_____
_____
_____

*Oh the weather outside is frightful, but the fire is so delightful, and since we've no place to go, let it snow! Let it snow! Let it snow!*

—*"Let It Snow"*

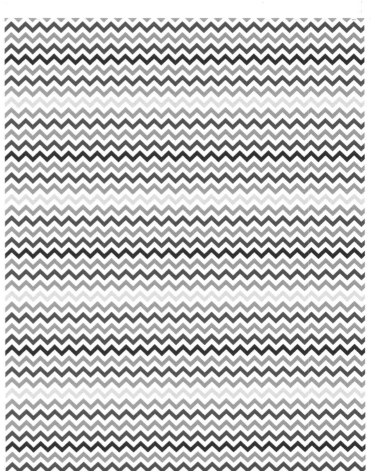

_____
_____
_____
_____
_____
_____
_____
_____

*Today's Christmas should mean creating happy hours for tomorrow and reliving those of yesterday.*

*—Gladys Taber*

_____
_____
_____
_____
_____

*Today's Christmas should mean creating happy hours for tomorrow and reliving those of yesterday.*

*—Gladys Taber*

_Peace on Earth will come to stay, when we live Christmas every day._

—_Helen Steiner Rice_

_Peace on Earth will come to stay, when we live Christmas every day._

—_Helen Steiner Rice_

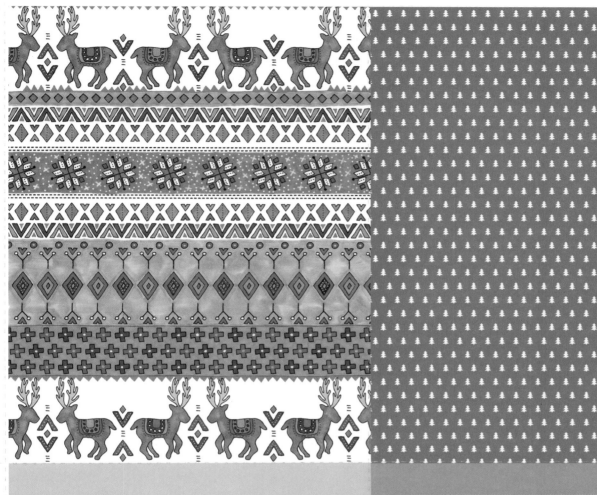

_____
_____
_____
_____
_____
_____
_____
_____

*Christmas isn't just a day,*
*it's a frame of mind.*

—*Miracle on 34th Street*

_____
_____
_____
_____
_____

*Christmas isn't just a day,*
*it's a frame of mind.*

—*Miracle on 34th Street*

_____

_____

_____

_____

_____

_____

_____

_____

*It's not what's under
the Christmas tree that matters.
It's who's around it.*

*—Unknown*

_____

_____

_____

_____

_____

*It's not what's under
the Christmas tree that matters.
It's who's around it.*

*—Unknown*

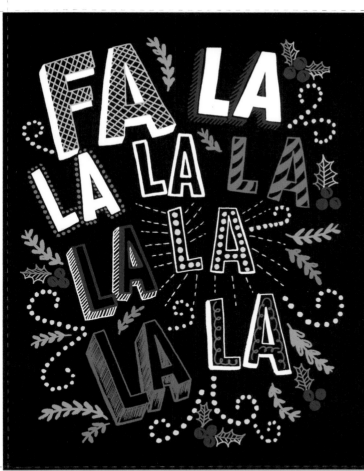

———————————————
———————————————
———————————————
———————————————
———————————————
———————————————
———————————————
———————————————

*It's beginning to look a lot like Christmas;*
*Soon the bells will start,*
*And the thing that will make them ring*
*Is the carol that you sing*
*Right within your heart.*

—Meredith Wilson, "It's Beginning to Look a
Lot Like Christmas"

———————————————
———————————————
———————————————
———————————————
———————————————

*It's beginning to look a lot like Christmas;*
*Soon the bells will start,*
*And the thing that will make them ring*
*Is the carol that you sing*
*Right within your heart.*

—Meredith Wilson, "It's Beginning to Look a
Lot Like Christmas"

_____

_____

_____

_____

_____

_____

_____

_____

*One of the most glorious messes in the world
is the mess created in the living room on
Christmas Day. Don't clean it up too quickly.*

*—Andy Rooney*

_____

_____

_____

_____

_____

*One of the most glorious messes in the world
is the mess created in the living room on
Christmas Day. Don't clean it up too quickly.*

*—Andy Rooney*

_____
_____
_____
_____
_____
_____
_____
_____

*At Christmas, play and make good cheer,*
*for Christmas comes but once a year.*

*—Thomas Tusser*

_____
_____
_____
_____
_____

*At Christmas, play and make good cheer,*
*for Christmas comes but once a year.*

*—Thomas Tusser*

_____
_____
_____
_____
_____
_____
_____
_____

*O Holy night, the stars are brightly shining*
*It is the night of our dear Savior's birth.*

— *"O Holy Night"*

_____
_____
_____
_____
_____

*O Holy night, the stars are brightly shining*
*It is the night of our dear Savior's birth.*

— *"O Holy Night"*

_____

_____

_____

_____

_____

_____

_____

*I hope your Christmas is as warm and sweet
as a cup of hot cocoa and filled with more
granted wishes than you can count.*

*—Unknown*

_____

_____

_____

_____

_____

*I hope your Christmas is as warm and sweet
as a cup of hot cocoa and filled with more
granted wishes than you can count.*

*—Unknown*

_____
_____
_____
_____
_____
_____
_____

*Rocking around the Christmas tree*
*Let the Christmas spirit ring*
*Later we'll have some pumpkin pie*
*and we'll do some caroling.*

*— "Rockin' Around the Christmas Tree"*

_____
_____
_____
_____
_____

*Rocking around the Christmas tree*
*Let the Christmas spirit ring*
*Later we'll have some pumpkin pie*
*and we'll do some caroling.*

*— "Rockin' Around the Christmas Tree"*

_____

_____

_____

_____

_____

_____

_____

*Perhaps the best Yuletide decoration
is being wreathed in smiles.*

*—Unknown*

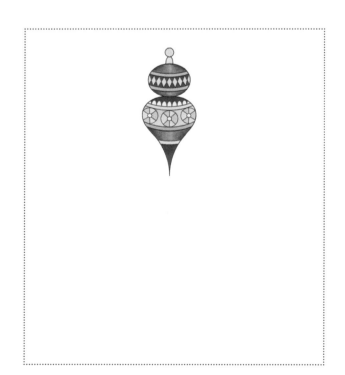

_____

_____

_____

_____

_____

*Perhaps the best Yuletide decoration
is being wreathed in smiles.*

*—Unknown*

_____
_____
_____
_____
_____
_____
_____
_____

*To make a winter friend*
*Find a carrot and some coal.*
*Gather up your friends*
*And roll a bunch of snow!*

*—Unknown*

_____
_____
_____
_____
_____

*To make a winter friend*
*Find a carrot and some coal.*
*Gather up your friends*
*And roll a bunch of snow!*

*—Unknown*

Just remove these two ready-to-roll cards and fold them down the middle!

_____
_____
_____
_____
_____

*Frosty the snowman*
*Was a jolly happy soul*
*With a corncob pipe and a button nose*
*And two eyes made out of coal*

*—"Frosty the Snowman"*

_____
_____
_____
_____
_____

*Frosty the snowman*
*Was a jolly happy soul*
*With a corncob pipe and a button nose*
*And two eyes made out of coal*

*—"Frosty the Snowman"*

Just remove these two ready-to-roll cards and fold them down the middle!

_____

_____

_____

_____

_____

*Christmas cookies and happy hearts,*
*this is how the holiday starts!*

*—Unknown*

_____

_____

_____

_____

_____

*Christmas cookies and happy hearts,*
*this is how the holiday starts!*

*—Unknown*

Just remove these two ready-to-roll cards and fold them down the middle!

*To appreciate the beauty of a snowflake,
it is necessary to stand out in the cold.*

*—Unknown*

*To appreciate the beauty of a snowflake,
it is necessary to stand out in the cold.*

*—Unknown*

Let your creativity loose with these colorable cards!

*Then the Grinch thought of
something he hadn't before!
What if Christmas, he thought,
doesn't come from a store.
What if Christmas, perhaps,
means a little bit more!*

*—Dr. Seuss,
How the Grinch Stole Christmas!*

*The best way to spread Christmas
cheer is singing loud for all to hear!*

*—Elf*

_____

_____

_____

_____

_____

*Then the Grinch thought of
something he hadn't before!
What if Christmas, he thought,
doesn't come from a store.
What if Christmas, perhaps,
means a little bit more!*

*—Dr. Seuss,
How the Grinch Stole Christmas!*

*The best way to spread Christmas
cheer is singing loud for all to hear!*

*—Elf*

Let your creativity loose with these colorable cards!

*Gifts of time and love*
*are surely the basic ingredients*
*of a truly merry Christmas.*

*—Peg Bracken*

*When it snows, ain't it thrilling,*
*though your nose gets a chilling,*
*we'll frolic and play,*
*the Eskimo way,*
*walking in a winter wonderland.*

*—"Winter Wonderland"*

_____

_____

_____

_____

_____

*Gifts of time and love*
*are surely the basic ingredients*
*of a truly merry Christmas.*

*—Peg Bracken*

*When it snows, ain't it thrilling,*
*though your nose gets a chilling,*
*we'll frolic and play,*
*the Eskimo way,*
*walking in a winter wonderland.*

*—"Winter Wonderland"*

Let your creativity loose with these colorable cards!

*I will honor Christmas in my heart,*
*and try to keep it all the year.*

*—Charles Dickens, A Christmas Carol*

*Jingle bells, jingle bells,*
*Jingle all the way.*
*Oh! what fun it is to ride*
*In a one-horse open sleigh.*

*—James Lord Pierpont, "Jingle Bells"*

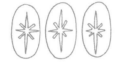

*I will honor Christmas in my heart,*
*and try to keep it all the year.*

*—Charles Dickens, A Christmas Carol*

*Jingle bells, jingle bells,*
*Jingle all the way.*
*Oh! what fun it is to ride*
*In a one-horse open sleigh.*

*—James Lord Pierpont, "Jingle Bells"*

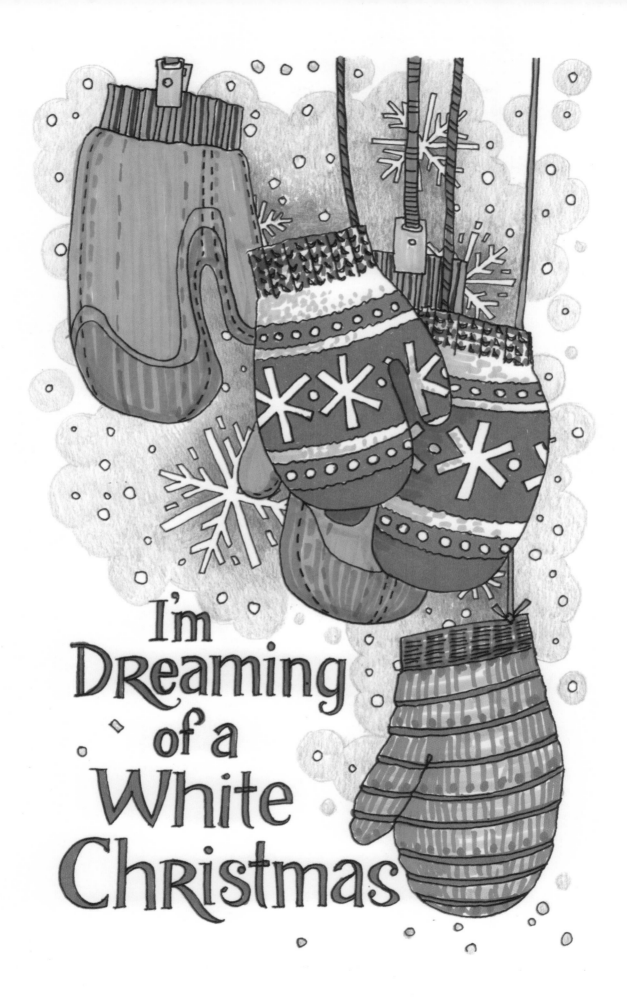

I'm Dreaming of a White Christmas

Always jingle all the way.

All the world is happy when Santa Claus comes.

—Maud Lindsay

Be filled with wonder. Be touched by peace.

JOYOUS · NOEL

A balanced diet is a Christmas cookie in each hand.

There are no strangers on Christmas Eve.

—Adele Comandini

At Christmas, all roads lead home.

—Marjorie Holmes

baby it's COLD Outside

Gloria, in excelsis Deo

—"Angels We Have Heard on High"

Don't get your tinsel in a tangle!

Every time a bell rings, an angel gets his wings.

—It's a Wonderful Life

Merry Christmas!

Happy Holidays!

It is Christmas in the heart that puts Christmas in the air.

—W. T. Ellis

Merry Christmas to all and to all a good night!

—'Twas the Night Before Christmas

Here we come a-caroling!

Celebrate the season.

'Tis the season

Share the Christmas spirit.

Happy New Year!

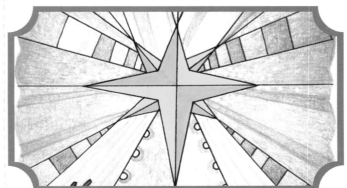

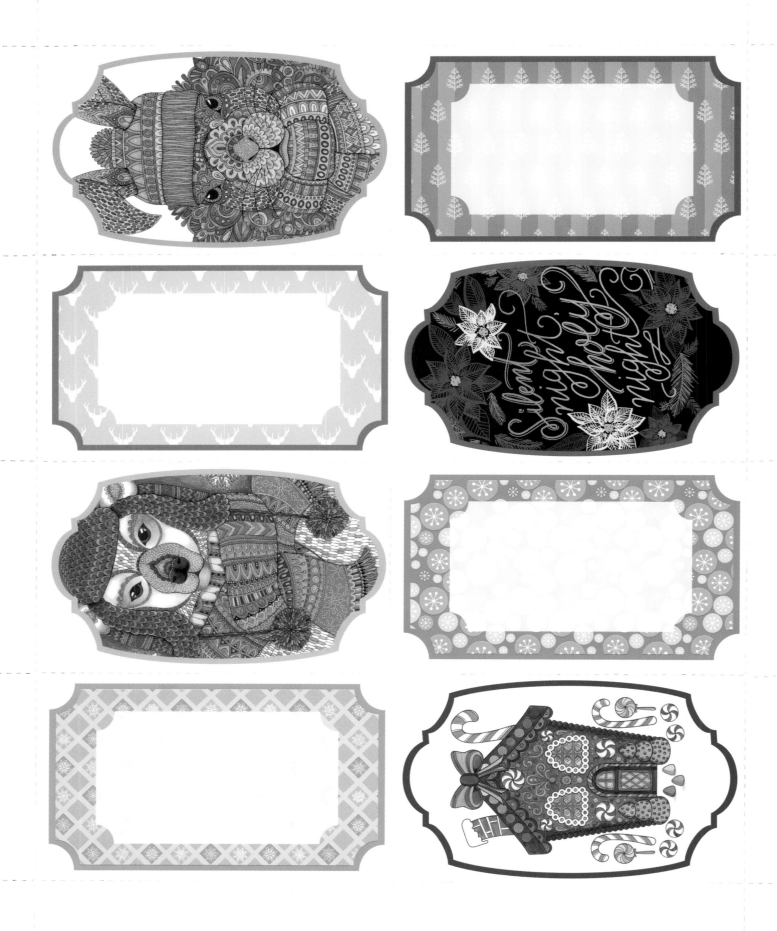

# Small Envelope Template - Cut out, trace, and reuse. Folding instructions on page 7.

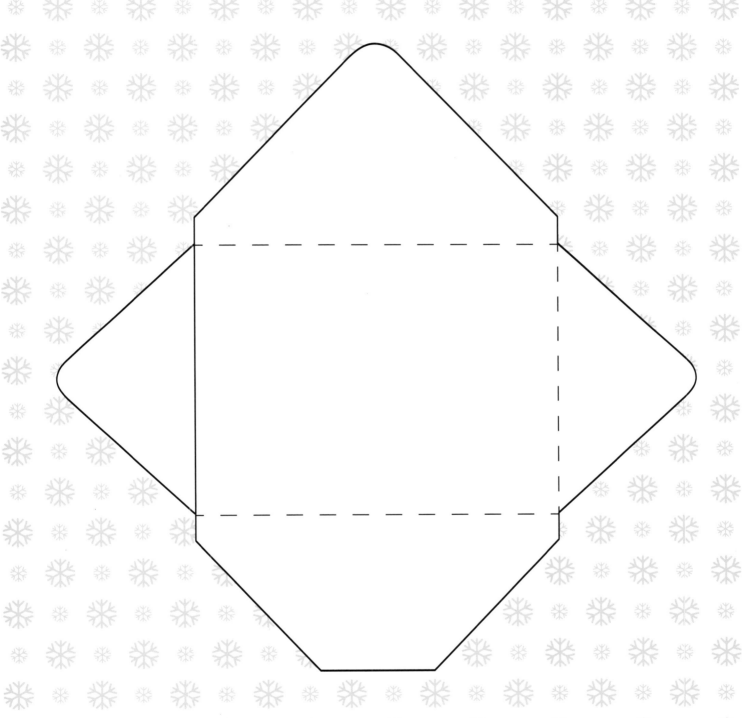

# Large Envelope Template
- Cut out, trace, and reuse. Folding instructions on page 7.

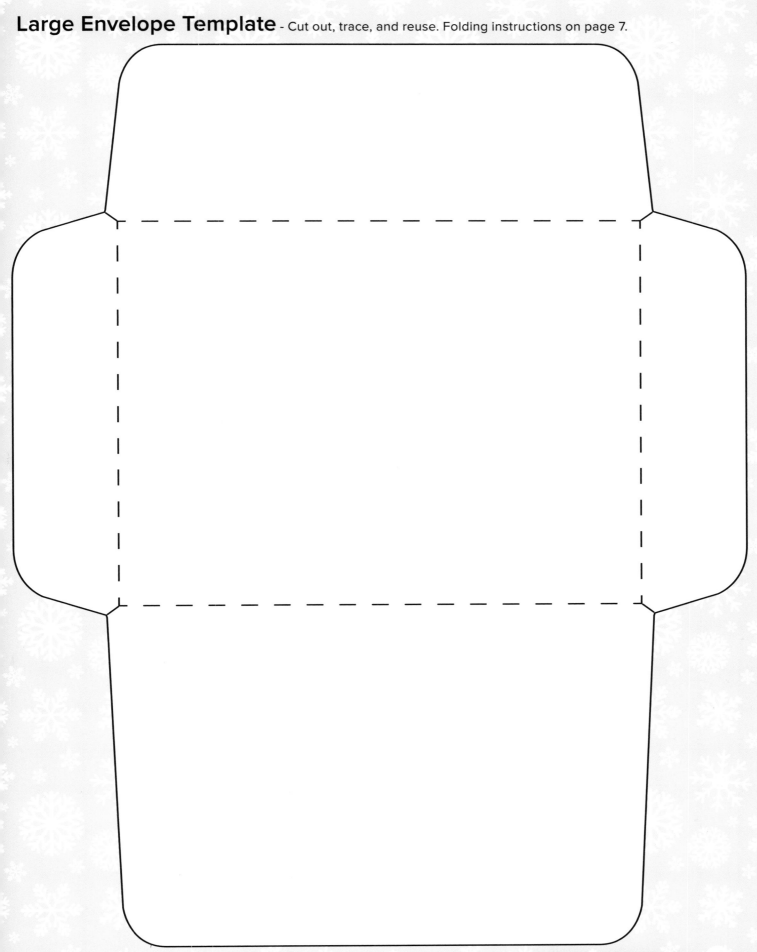

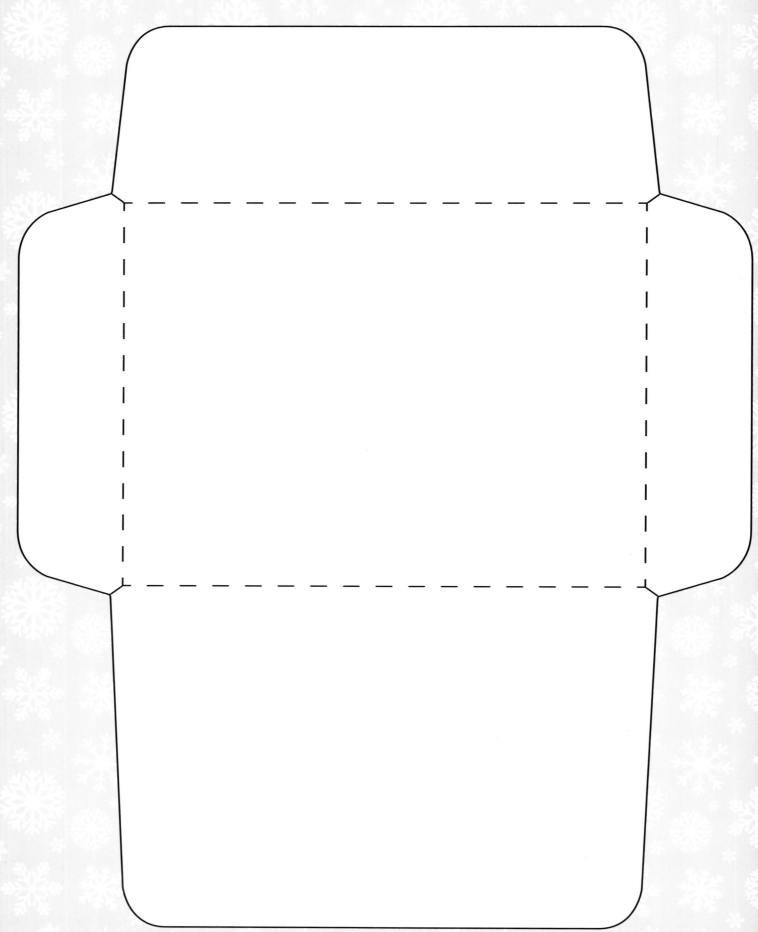

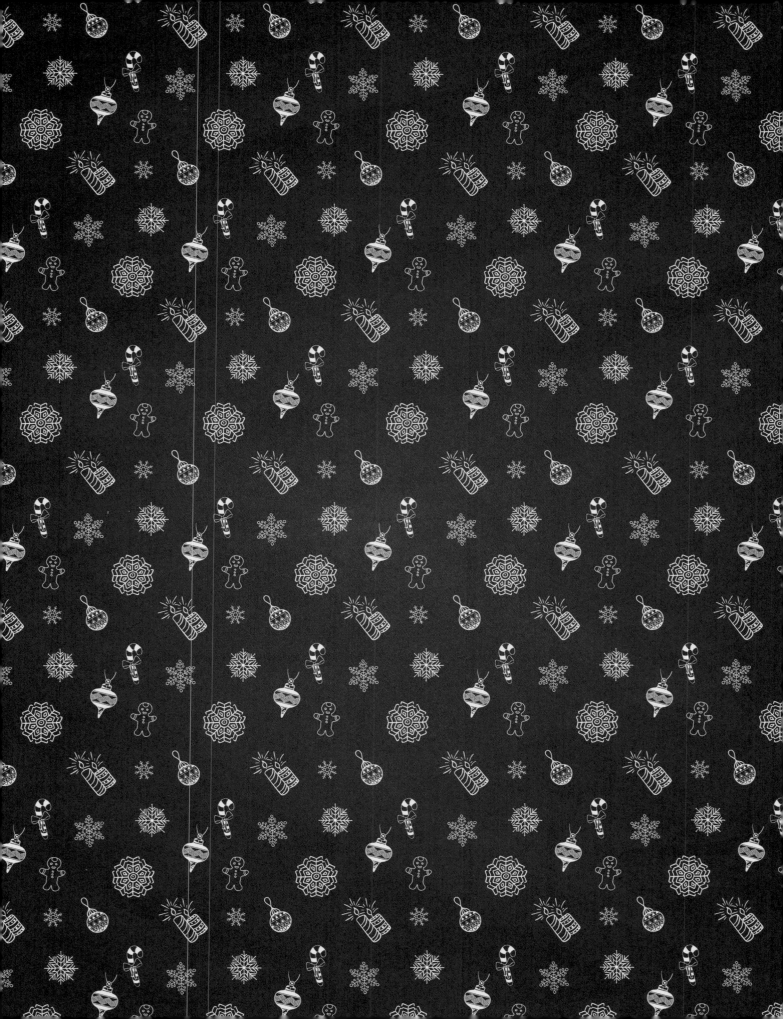